A is for Angelina Jolie.
She stepped onto the world
stage as an Oscar-winning
Hollywood starlet, but then
became known for lending
a hand to those in need,
visiting more than 20 countries
to help fight for the rights
of refugees. Legendary
lefty empathy!

Bb

B is for Ruth **B**ader Ginsburg. The Notorious RBG is one of many lefties known for having a gift for language. In 1993, she became the second ever female Supreme Court justice, and has been a leading voice for civil rights and gender equality ever since!

C is for Marie and Pierre **C**urie. This legendary left-handed husband and wife duo helped solve huge scientific mysteries through their creative thinking. They shared half the 1903 Nobel Prize for Physics, with Marie adding a Nobel Prize in Chemistry in 1911. Absolute marriage goals!

D is for **D**iego Maradona. Small in size but gigantic in stature, The Golden Boy's magical left foot stopped right-footed opponents in their tracks. And who can forget his controversial left 'hand of God' goal at the 1986 World Cup?!

E is for **El**vis Costello. This Rock and Roll Hall of Famer was a lefty through and through: "I'm totally left-sided. I am completely left-handed, completely left-footed." One of many left-handed musical geniuses, Costello helped shape the sound of Rock and Roll.

F is for Will **F**errell. This super creative lefty is one of the funniest comedic actors of his generation. Ferrell is the man behind all-time classic movie characters like Ron Burgundy, Ricky Bobby and Buddy the Elf. Stay classy, lefty legends!

G is for Bill **G**ates. His incredible intelligence led him to create Microsoft, one of the world's biggest companies. But what's truly legendary is this left-handed billionaire's generous philanthropy: both he and wife Melinda have donated more than $40 billion to charities around the world.

H is for Jimi Hendrix. When his father wanted him to play right-handed, this groovy guitar genius became ambidextrous, re-stringing his righty Fender Stratocasters so he could play them left-handed. This mixed-handedness unlocked some legendary playing.

I is for **I**saac Newton. Many believe Newton was a lefty, which was considered a bad thing in the 1600s and 1700s. But this mastermind persevered through bullying at school to become a scientific genius whose Laws of Motion helped lay the foundation for modern science.

Jj

J is for Jerry Seinfeld and Jason Alexander. These two lefty besties are unforgettable as Jerry and George on the 1990s hit sitcom 'Seinfeld' where they spent a lot of time talking about ... nothing. Not that there's anything wrong with that!

K is for Helen **K**eller. Born both deaf and blind, this inspiring lady still learned how to read, write and type. With her left hand, she read braille, and enjoyed music by feeling vibrations from record players and singers' throats and lips. Truly extraordinary!

L is for David **L**etterman and Jay Leno. Like many southpaws, these two lefty late night legends saw the world a bit differently. Their quips and punchlines made for decades of amusing television and helped millions of viewers end their day with a laugh.

M is for Marilyn Monroe. This lefty lived life on her own terms, saying, "If I'd observed all the rules, I'd never have got anywhere." Unafraid to make a splash on and off the big screen in the 1950s, Monroe is an eternal Hollywood icon.

N is for Martina **N**avratilova. One of the best tennis players ever, Navratilova surprised many opponents with her left-handed serve and volley attack. These moves gave her a huge advantage on the court and helped her win 18 Grand Slam titles during her amazing career.

Oo

O is for Barack Obama. Fighting adversity and staying flexible in the face of challenges, the 44th U.S. President brought hope to millions. Interestingly, four out of the five U.S. Presidents between 1981 and 2016 were left-handed!

P is for **P**aul McCartney. This loveable lefty lad from Liverpool is one of the best and most successful musicians ever. Sir Paul and drummer Ringo Starr were both south-paws whose creativity helped The Beatles become the biggest and most influential band in history.

Qq

Q is for Queen Elizabeth, the Queen Mother. Alongside her husband, King George VI, this British matriarch helped lead the United Kingdom from 1936–1952. She was a source of strength and compassion to her nation and her family, including her daughter, Queen Elizabeth II.

R is for Babe **R**uth.
By hitting a then-record
714 home runs, this legendary
baseball player earned
many nicknames: The Great
Bambino, The Colossus of
Clout and The Sultan of Swat.
A feared batter, Ruth actually
started his career as
a southpaw pitcher.

S is for **S**tan Lee.
That's right, true believers!
It was with a creative left
hand that Stan 'The Man'
Lee brought to life some
of the most legendary comic
book heroes in the universe!
Spider-Man, Daredevil and
the Avengers – Excelsior!

T is for Harry S. **T**ruman. Like many of his generation, Truman was forced to write with his right hand in school even though he was a lefty. But his legendary perseverance helped him overcome early issues with writing and speaking, and he went on to become the 33rd U.S. President!

U is for **U**ri Geller.
He's the southpaw magician who has entertained audiences around the world for decades. And while some don't believe in his on-stage tricks, there's no doubting this showman's mastery of sleight of hand. Blink and you might miss it!

V is for Leonardo da **V**inci. Legendary artist, inventor and all-around genius, da Vinci produced some of the most stunning artwork the world has ever seen. The 'Mona Lisa' and 'The Last Supper' are just two of his masterpieces.

Ww

W is for Oprah **W**infrey. So much more than a talk show host, The Queen of All Media is a true global influencer. Over her illustrious career, she has inspired a whole generation, and donated hundreds of millions of dollars to charity along the way.

X is for Sandy Koufax.
Batters weren't used to lefty
pitchers, let alone Koufax's
legendary delivery! Considered
the best southpaw pitcher in
baseball history, The Left Arm
of God was the first to throw
four no-hitters and win three
Cy Young Awards!

Yy

Y is for Steve **Y**oung. This two-time football MVP was the first lefty quarterback inducted into the Hall of Fame. He's known as much for his great passing as for his legendary running ability, which helped introduce the art of the rushing quarterback.

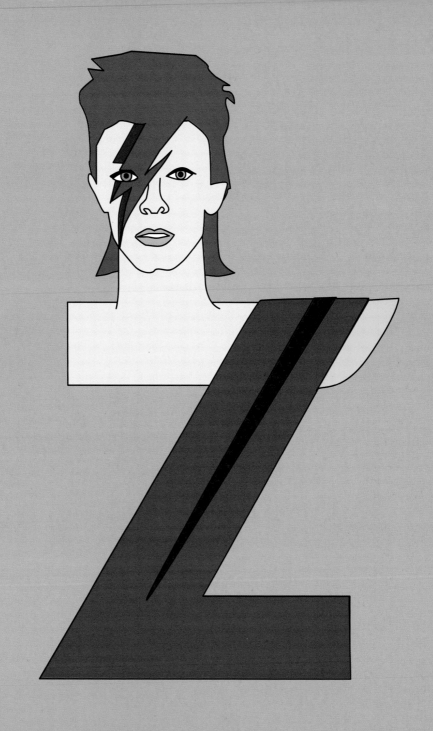

Z is for **Z**iggy Stardust. When it comes to creative lefties, few can top David Bowie and his alter ego Ziggy Stardust. His cosmic sound and enchanting outfits made Bowie a one-of-a-kind rock legend. A Space Oddity, to say the least!

The ever-expanding legendary library

EXPLORE THESE LEGENDARY ALPHABETS & MORE AT WWW.ALPHABETLEGENDS.COM

LEFT-HANDED LEGENDS ALPHABET
www.alphabetlegends.com

Published by Alphabet Legends Pty Ltd in 2020
Created by Beck Feiner
Copyright © Alphabet Legends Pty Ltd 2020

UNICEF AUSTRALIA
A portion of the Net Proceeds from the sale of this book
are donated to UNICEF.

9780648962809

ALPHABET LEGENDS